T0130090

IN MOM'S HOUSE

IN MOM'S HOUSE

A MEMOIR

ELAIN L EDGE

iUniverse, Inc.
Bloomington

In Mom's House
A Memoir

iUniverse books may be ordered through booksellers or by contacting:

iUniverse
1663 Liberty Drive
Bloomington, IN 47403
www.iuniverse.com
1-800-Authors (1-800-288-4677)

ISBN: 978-1-4759-3740-4 (sc)
ISBN: 978-1-4759-3741-1 (ebk)

Printed in the United States of America

iUniverse rev. date: 07/24/2012

Iowa gets really hot and steamy in August. In the years when farmers were struggling to make a living as the country was just coming out of the big depression, and before the advent of huge farm machinery, they worked together as neighborhoods while harvesting, etc. So, on the 22nd day of August in 1932, the neighbors gathered at our farm to thresh the oats from the straw. The task of feeding the 10-12 hungry, hard working men fell to the farm wives. Not only was the noon meal which included meat, potatoes, vegetables, bread, butter and dessert expected, but an afternoon lunch of sandwiches, cookies and lemonade or homemade root beer was to be prepared and carried to the fields each day. The main dishes for the noon meal were cooked on the kitchen cook stove, a large, heavy piece of equipment, which had an iron top with four round removable grates separating the wood and cob fire from the cooking surface. The bread would have been baked that morning in the hot oven which was the lower part of the large stove. In August, the kitchen heat was sometimes almost unbearable. Yet, I'm sure that my mother embraced the task of the food preparation without complaining, because she believed one was to just do what one had to do and whining about it wouldn't make it easier. She may have had a "hired girl" for that day, and I feel confident that Muriel, my ten year old sister would have been helping in the kitchen as well. Eight year old LaVon was most likely occupied entertaining six year old Ellwood and four year old Arleen, although there would have been tasks for them as well, according to each of his or her capabilities. They no doubt had pumped drinking water from the well and carried it into the house. Some of the food would have had to have been kept cool, so they would have carried the sealed jars full of fruit or coleslaw to the cooling tank which was connected to the watering tank for the cattle and horses by a steel pipe. Surely, the younger children had collected the cobs from the cob house or wood from the wood pile for the stove. Work in mom's house was a family affair, and no one expected anything different.

Some hours later, Dad would have left to pick up the midwife, because I was born into that family the next morning at 6:00 A.M. It is doubtful that I was a planned baby, however, I could have been since two years before almost to the day, a baby son had been born and died two weeks later. Years later, I heard an old fashioned farm wife explain that she was elated when her daughter had been born because she would finally get some help. Her husband, she explained, had been blessed with two sons to help him, while her work load had only increased to care for them, but now, because her daughter had been born, she would also have some help. If that had been my parent's philosophy, my conception might have been planned with hopes to replace the son who had not lived.

Since both of my Norwegian grandmothers were named Inger, the one who was still living thought that should also be my name. However, Mom and Dad thought giving an "old fashioned" name to me was not the thing to do. Perhaps they just didn't know how to spell it, since Mom was educated only to the fourth grade, and spelled purely phonetically and left the unnecessary e off the end of my name.

One of the family's often told stories was that mom's talkative friend, Genevieve, picked me up and began talking in her complimentary fashion when she came to welcome me at the age of four days. I looked at her and began to make happy baby noises in response. Ellwood often told the story as, "Elain started talking at four days, and she hasn't stopped since." That story was not disputed by my parents or the older girls, so I assume it was true.

OVERVIEW

We were poor, but I never realized it since all of our friends and relatives lived very much the way that we did. That included raising and butchering our own meat animals, and milking our own cows. The large jars of fresh milk and cream were stored in the cooling tank which was fed from well water. One of the unpleasant tasks was washing the separator. The milk was poured into a huge stainless steel bowl and with the help of one person turning a handle, the cream would flow out of one spout and the "non-fat" milk would be routed into another spout. We would have delicious whipping cream, with some of that made into butter by turning the handle of a butter churn—again by hand and muscle. We often made ice cream by mixing eggs, cream, sugar, flavoring, and sometimes fresh or canned fruit. The mix was then poured into a stainless steel cylinder, placed in the wooden bucket, then surrounded by chopped ice and coarse salt before attaching a paddle type churner into the cream mixture. It was then topped with a cover attached to a device that held it in place, and allowed the churning job to be accomplished by turning a wooden handle for a very long time. The mixture would then turn into the frozen delicious treat. Some of the rich cream was allowed to sour, which became a special dish when served over a thick slice of homemade bread and sprinkled with sugar. That dish was a stark contrast to milk toast which was warm milk poured over a thick slice of toasted bread, and served to us when we felt "puny." We toasted the bread over the open flame in the cook stove, after removing one of the grates on the stove top. If it became blackened or a bit charred, we were told that eating the burned parts would make us good singers.

As soon as we were old enough to know weeds from plants, we helped in our huge garden. One day, Dad and I were planting. We had planted several rows of peas, and I told Dad I thought that was enough since I hated podding the peas. He agreed, and we threw the remainder of the pea seeds to the chickens. Mom was irate when she discovered what we had done. Thinking we could fool her was really not possible, nor did she accept the fact that I thought a task was too tedious.

Mom raised chickens big time, and seemed to love doing it. A mad rooster had attacked me one time when I was exploring the chicken yard, so I was deathly afraid of the chickens. I hated the smell of the chicken house also. Mom taught her brood of children to work as an assembly line dressing them when the chickens were big enough to eat, before she home canned them. Later, as her flocks increased, she sold extras for income. Ellwood and I were on the "defeathering" detail. If this was a day to butcher chickens, Dad or Mom would catch the required number of "fryers" by going into the chicken house with the chicken catcher, which was a long wire with a hook on one end. They would sneak up on the chicken, hook the catcher onto one of the legs and drag it out of the chicken house. Mom would pick up the bird by the head, and vigorously twist the head **until** it came off—(much easier than chopping it off with an axe???) She then would throw the chicken into the yard where it would flop around until the nerves died. Next, Ellwood would dip it into boiling water to make it possible for he and I to pull off the feathers by the handful. He would slowly turn the naked bird back and forth over a bon fire to "singe" the skin before the next step. The other kids could pull out the innards and cut up the chicken to frying pieces. That assembly line was efficient and we could do several chickens in a morning. However, it had its drawbacks. When

I got married, it was assumed I would follow the traditional farm wives from both families and raise chickens to eat. So, during Norman's and my first spring as a young married couple, we ordered several dozen baby roosters to boost our meat supply. When they were big enough to eat, the two of us tried to dress the first bird. Norman chopped the head off with an axe, as he thought that was more humane. Getting the feathers off was no problem. However, neither of us knew what to do next. Somehow, our experimenting got the job done, but we had the strangest pieces of chicken to eat. I knew I would never raise hens, since I hated picking eggs. I don't remember ever being "Pecked" while getting the egg from under the hen, however my Grandma Sandven's hands bore several scars from that task. My assertive nature really took root the following spring when I made the decision never to raise chickens ever again.

Mom's hens that were no longer laying and had begun to molt, were culled out and cooked, then eaten with homemade noodles for a delicious meal. Her chickens were fed well, so the fat hens were a real treat. Sometimes, the feet were cleaned and cooked also. That grizzle made for a tasty treat.

Once a week, we would go to Hardy to "trade" our farm produce, especially eggs, for staples at the grocery store. During the summer, "trading" usually occurred on the same day that the free show was scheduled. A "cowboy "movie would be projected up on a big screen in the center of the town where we sat to watch on benches made from planks held up by drain tiles. We would leave home early so we could be assured of having a prime parking place where Mom could sit and watch the movie. We kids would join her there on rainy or chilly nights, but it was more fun to sit with our friends. My high school principal would later explain that we watched the same set of rocks being shot up every time we went to the cowboy movies.

We played cards around the kitchen table almost every night. Consequently, we learned about number values early in our lives. Rook and Five Hundred were our favorite games. Mom loved to play cards, and was very competitive. If she was having bad luck, she would get up and walk around her chair, as an old wives' tale allowed her to believe that action would change her luck. If it appeared that she had been dealt a winning hand, she would exclaim, "If I don't make this bid, I'll eat my shoes." We kids would sometimes play Chinese checkers and Monopoly if we had time to kill during the day. During the summer months, we played croquet on our level big outdoor houseyard.

Every Saturday night, whether we needed it or not—that's a joke—we had baths in the round granite bathtub. Some of the older kids would carry water that had been pumped up from the well into the house, and it would be heated on the cook stove to a temperature comfortable for a bath. The big tub would sit in the corner of the kitchen and we took turns getting into it one at a time. The clean person would wipe with a towel and dress in clean pajamas, then the next person would enter the kitchen, etc. The water got pretty scummy with soap and dirt residue by the end of the night when it was finally dumped outside, preferably on a place where weeds grew, as the soap scum was to act as a weed killer. I don't think the water was ever completely changed between kids, but sometimes a pail of hotter water would be poured into it so the last few didn't have cold baths.

RELIGOUS TRAINING

Sunday mornings ALWAYS found our family in church at Lake Lutheran. I don't remember any of us even suggesting that we not go. My first pastor had been part of that congregation for a very long time, and so—he was also part of my family's life. I thought of him as a judge rather than a compassionate person. He served two parishes, Samuel Lutheran in Eagle Grove and the one in Lake Township. One Sunday, as he concluded his sermon, he announced that since he had a meeting that afternoon with our congregation, he would ask one of "our good families," if he could have dinner with them, so he didn't have to drive back to Eagle Grove and right back again. Sure enough, he looked right at my family. As soon as we got in the car, Mom and Dad announced we should hurry home and hide the Sunday paper, since Rev. Severtson wouldn't like it if he knew we had engaged in such a worldly activity as reading the paper on Sunday. Nevertheless, Mom didn't like preaching at people. She believed one should live their religious convictions, not talk openly about them.

Dad had two brothers who were preachers. Uncle Johnny was ordained and quite revered by his siblings, although we didn't see him very often while growing up. Uncle Clarence, who was a self-proclaimed "tent evangelist," came to our house every year when he came to Eagle Grove to set up his tent and have "meetings." It was quite evident that Mom tolerated him and his wife Mary, and would prepare an annual meal for

5

them, but it was also evident that she did not like his style of preaching. They would come in one of the latest models of a new car and she felt he begged money from those who attended his "meetings." He prayed very long prayers for "Ephraim's family coming to know the Lord," before eating the annual meal. Mom believed her style of Christianity made a bigger difference in the world. It was not uncommon to find her after our noon meal taking a break by reading from the Bible, but her philosophy mirrored the St. Francis of Assisi's statement that I have on my wall—"Preach the gospel at all times, and when necessary use words."

Sunday School preceded the worship service in the basement of Lake Lutheran. The one big room was divided into grade level sections by brown canvas curtains which were strung from wires criss crossing the space a couple of feet below the ceiling. It served the purpose well since none of the students "acted up." We learned the Bible Stories well, so I knew about Jesus Christ from the time I was a small child, but only learned to know Him in a personal way while a student at Waldorf College.

We spent two years studying preconfirmation doctrine, which Mom called "Reading for the Preacher." However, the only time we "read" for him was if he handed something out on paper in one of the sessions. Luther's Small Catechism was memorized by heart. Once a week, Mom would call whichever child was of the ages 11-13 to her side to "hear our lessons." The study book had an outline form where a particular part of the catechism was presented, followed by "what does this mean? That part had to be memorized word for word. Two pages of questions referring to that text would follow, the question printed in black bold type and the answer in blue italics. I learned to roller skate back and forth from the back porch steps to the gate, repeating the blue answer one question at a time, until I knew those answers perfectly to meet Mom's standard. Occasionally, she might elaborate a bit on the answer, but didn't allow our recitation to stray from the written word. After the two years of "reading" was finished it was time for confirmation. It took place in two parts. I still cringe as I remember the night when my classmates and I lined up and down the aisles of Lake Lutheran, where we were questioned by the pastor while the congregation listened to hear which mother's child was best prepared to answer word for word. The next step was the conference with the pastor. I was extremely nervous as I entered his small study to the side of the altar. He quizzed me about the lessons, and then said, "Elain, are you a Christian?" 'Of course,' I thought. "What does he think, that I've just learned all this stuff because I needed something to do?" I answered "Yes," and then he said, "How do you know?" It had never dawned on me to NOT know, but I didn't know how to answer. He kindly said, "I believe you are, but you should know the reason, and it is because you believe God loves you and sent his Son to die for your sins."

Lutherans pride themselves as singing with gusto. At least we did at Lake Lutheran. Along with the lesson for each part of the catechism, there was a hymn to memorize. I still may catch myself singing the words I learned from a familiar hymn rather than the modernized version. That always drove Norman a bit crazy, and I would remind him that I was signing to God, not to him or the persons sitting in front of us. No one had even heard of "With One Voice," or argued about what color the hymn book should be in that day. Most small churches had stretched their budgets to buy the old green books as it was. A hymn board was hung at the side of the pulpit which was made with grooves for the hymn numbers to be displayed guiding the congregation to the correct page. Agnes Sampson sat on the piano bench and accompanied the singing. Marilyn Gangstead was in my confirmation class and she played the piano quite well also. She and I became friends, and the two of us sang duets often as special music, and usually sang for funerals within the congregation.

Marilyn and I also became the Daily Vacation Bible School Teachers when we were older high school youth. I'm sure our pupils got a very sketchy education for those two weeks. Since the cemetery surrounds the church, we played hide and seek with our pupils at recess time behind the tomb stones. After that summer, Rev. Severtson gave each of us a leather bound "Concordia Hymn Book."

After confirmation, we were eligible to attend Luther League. Even older siblings who were still living at home attended those Sunday night events. One thing that was standard for the beginning of the meeting was to answer roll call by repeating a memorized Bible verse. Ellwood consistently answered," In God was light, and in him is no darkness at all." (I John:1-5) I'm sorry that we did not include that verse in his funeral service.

EXTENDED FAMILY

We spent nearly every Sunday afternoon at Grandma Sandven's home. Grandpa Sandven walked with crutches. Eventually, one of his feet had to be amputated from lack of circulation. My memories of him were that of a kind man who was generous to us according to his meager means. He had emigrated from Norway when he was 17 years old, and was met in the United States by his older sister. He had farming roots in Norway, but spent part of his early years in the US as a tailor. Inger Olson had been born in Illinois, and traveled with her family by covered wagon to the Thor, Iowa area. It was there that the two met, as Inger's father was also a tailor. Since readymade clothing was expensive beyond new immigrant's means, it was beneficial if people knew how to make their own. Later, Grandpa Sandven farmed and raised cattle and hogs for slaughter. His children told stories of "herding cattle to Thor" on foot where the cattle were then put on train cars and shipped to Chicago to be sold for meat. My mother fondly remembered his homecomings from those trips as he often brought nice gifts for his children. She had a beautiful gold ring which had a ruby set in the center, flanked on each side by a row of seed pearls. I loved that ring!! In one of her tender moments, she gifted each of her then adult daughters with one of those souvenirs. That beautiful ring was mine!! It was much too delicate to wear while washing dishes, so I had the habit of taking it off for that task and placing it in the kitchen window sill. I forgot about it when we began to remodel our kitchen in the big brick house in which Norman and I raised our children. We sifted several bushels of kitchen rubble in an effort to find that ring to no avail. I never had the heart to tell Mom, and each time I enter an antique shop yet today, I search the jewelry counter for a copy of that ring.

Aunt Amy, my mother's younger sister was everyone's favorite. She was saddled with the job of teaching each of us girls how to play the piano. How she must have hated spending Sunday afternoons teaching her nieces when she spent the entire week teaching school, but she never let on that we were a burden. She played one song on the piano that we always asked her to play. She would trill the keys to make them sound like a bird in the rendition of "Listen to the Mockingbird." She had a snazzy tan colored Ford coupe with a rumble seat in the back. It would be a special treat for us to go for a ride in the rumble seat. No one had ever heard about seat belts, but Aunt Amy never drove very fast, and I don't think anyone thought we were in danger.

Grandpa Haaland lived in Eagle Grove, and would occasionally drive to our farm to visit. However, he spoke only Norwegian, so he usually visited with only Dad and Mom, while we kids would catch only a word here and there. My parents were anxious for us to live in the modern USA, not the "old country" so we were not encouraged to learn to speak Norwegian. Mom and Dad would occasionally speak it to each other when they didn't want us kids to know what they were saying. Grandma Haaland had died when Dad was a young boy. Since she left five small children, Grandpa remarried a short time later. His new wife bore him only one more child, a daughter, my Aunt Ida. That wife also died as a young woman, perhaps from overwork, taking care of her own baby along with the four young sons and one daughter who had become her new family when she married.

We lived close to our cousins, and they were our best friends during our early childhood. Uncle Levi and Aunt Pearl also spent many Sundays at

Grandma Sandven's and Dad had started farming working with Uncle Levi, so their children were very close cousins. Gib and Dorothy were closest to me in age, and we spent hours playing house along with my sister, Arleen. My favorite time of the year was late summer when the small orchard on their acreage was producing. Since we didn't have apple and plum trees or raspberry bushes at home, we usually came home with bags full of fruit. Our Sunday night suppers at Grandma's house always included sauce made from some of the fruit. It also would include some kind of meat, and my grandma's homemade bread. A specialty was head cheese, which was made from cooking the head of a butchered animal, and then extracting the particles of meat which were stuck into small crevices. It was a jellied consistency and was really quite good.

Dad and Uncle Levi worked together with butchering pigs or steers for meat. They made a sausage that was delicious. The small sausage grinder sat on the floor. One of them would feed a bowl type receptacle with chunks of meat which had been blended with spices, while the other would turn the handle and the sausage would come out of a spout encased in a gut like casing. It was then canned in jars, and cold packed to preserve it. It was delicious!! Chickens and chunks of beef were canned in that same way, but they would save some of the beef to dry it. Mom had a wonderful recipe for dried beef, and continued to make it throughout her life. It would still be my favorite food, I'm sure, if I could find someone to make it. Late in her life, she would sometimes give us each a "hunk" of dried beef for Christmas. I always hid it, and ate most of the piece myself without sharing it with Norman or my kids. Some of the home butchering sounds pretty gross in today's frame of mind, but it was accepted as part of our daily life, and we thought nothing of it. Blood pudding was made by putting a strip of suet into a stocking like casing, then filling it with the blood of the butchered animal, and I don't know what else. After if coagulated and cooled, it was sliced and fried in grease for an evening meal. Rendering the lard was one process that almost made me sick. The fat from the pigs would be sliced off while the animal was hanging to "cure" from a tree, then brought into the house. Mom would use her large oblong granite roaster to heat the fat in the oven until the liquid lard was separated from the cracklings. It filled the whole house with a pungent smell, which lasted for several days. However, to this day, I believe the best pie crust is made from lard, but I'm thankful I can buy a one pound package and don't have to render it. Part of the fat was also made into soap, being mixed with a lye solution. That was used for laundry, but not for our weekly baths as it was strong and would have chapped our skin.

Since we lived close to Hardy where Dad's brother, Uncle Eddie, and Aunt Alma lived with their family, I was tolerated by my cousin, Ruth and sister Arleen who were about the same age. We often visited my dad's sister, Aunt Marie and her husband Uncle Ed Sadler. They lived in Eagle Grove where Uncle Ed worked on a railroad crew. They had ten children in a house which had been made from two passenger rail cars. Mary Ellen and Russ were my favorite playmates from that family. I loved the few times I spent overnight with them, because we slept in bunk beds that lined the narrow aisle, and we could go "swimming" in the real pool which was close to them. I was jealous that those cousins all learned to swim at an early age, while I was afraid of the water, and only became an intermediate swimmer after age thirty.

Most of our social contacts were family and close neighbors. A very rare "outing" was a trip to the Iowa State Fair with Uncle Levi's family. Even in that time, the annual event drew a lot of people, and being in crowds was a pretty foreign feeling to me. I wandered away from my family and after a while, I began to realize I was surrounded by a sea of people whom I did not know. As I write this, I can vividly remember the panicked feeling, which vanished when I heard my Aunt Pearl call out, "Here she is," and I ran into her arms.

HARDSHIPS

During the summer when I was four, Barbara and Duane, two of the Sadler cousins were spending time at our farm. Since our family raised food, it was common for some of Aunt Marie's brood to spend part of the summer at our farm. That year, their visit was interrupted when one of my siblings came down with a high fever and a very sore throat. Scarlet fever!! I don't remember which sibling got sick first, but LaVon and I didn't get it until the others were nearly well. Families with scarlet fever were quarantined by the state health authorities in an effort to keep the disease from spreading throughout the whole population. Soon after the kids in our family got sick, Mom also came down with the dreaded fever and sore throat, so most of our house was turned into a hospital like setting with Muriel, Ellwood, Arleen, and Mom lying in makeshift beds throughout the house. I remember that the fever had drastic effects on the older kids, and Ellwood, at one time, had been "out of his head, "which caused a panic in the family.

Doc Basinger, our doctor from Goldfield, made a house call and brought large syringes of a new medicine. Mom didn't have much faith in Doc Basinger, and often said he was fine if you told him what was wrong with you and didn't need a diagnosis. However, I imagine she was pretty desperate to help the family get better. Perhaps Dad drove to Goldfield to explain the situation to him, since telephones were rarely if ever in rural homes at that time. LaVon and I were to stay in the kitchen away from those who were sick. Dad and the hired man slept in the barn and were to stay out of the house which was quarantined from the healthy population. My fifth birthday occurred during this time, and I had requested a chocolate cake with burned sugar frosting. LaVon, the thirteen year old sister, did her best to satisfy my request. Perhaps I was getting sick when my big day arrived, because I could not eat it, and I don't know if anyone else could as well. However, soon both LaVon and I also became sick. I believe the large shots must have been the precursor to penicillin because I broke out with hives in addition to the fever and sore throat. Penicillin does that to me yet today. A neighbor, "Dutch", brought watermelon which actually tasted good. Mom had not been a fan of Dutch, since he was apparently an alcoholic, not understood by me, however, she welcomed the watermelon gift as it was one of the few foods that I would eat during that time. The family had already been quarantined for weeks, and now that time was extended until LaVon and I were free of contagion. Needless to say, our recuperating siblings were not happy, and often reminded us of that. After six long weeks, the house had to be scrubbed from top to bottom, and then fumigated with strong smelling candles before it was declared free from disease.

Dad rented farm land, and March 1 was traditionally moving day among farmers who rented land from land owners. That year, following the scarlet fever experience, we moved farther north in Humboldt County near Livermore, another small town. We moved into a large old wooden frame house. The older girls rode the school bus every day to Vernon Consolidated High School, while Ellwood and Arleen attended a one room rural school about one half mile from our new farm.

The house had an apartment upstairs where our hired man, his wife Beulah, and baby Donnie lived. On March 28, a very windy morning, Beulah had bathed Donnie and put him down for a nap, and had come downstairs to visit with Mom. They were frightened when they noticed flames rising up outside the window. Looking out of the door, we saw that the outside stairway leading to the apartment was engulfed in flames. Beulah began to scream that her baby would burn, and ran up the inside stairway. Mom yelled at me to run to our neighbors, the Kubly's, and have them call the fire department since we didn't yet have a telephone. I started down the steep hill toward their house, but the Kubly's son, Leonard, who later became LaVon's husband, was already running toward our house, and said his mother had called the fire department because they had seen the flames. Mom was outside waving a white dishtowel as she saw Dad's team of horses approaching our direction. The white dishtowel was our "cell phone" from the house to the field. Mom and Leonard immediately began carrying furniture out of the house, and an oft repeated story was that the two of them had carried an oak buffet full of dishes with a gas lamp sitting on top of it out of the house so successfully, that they had only broken one tea cup. Our yard soon filled with cars from neighbors, or people from throughout the "section" of land who had noticed the fire. Mom brought Donnie to me, who had been put down to nap in the nude. She took us to a far corner of the house yard, and firmly instructed me to "sit here and hang on to Donnie. Don't let him up for anything," she said. Donnie was a pretty hefty one year old, while I was a small five year old whom Ellwood had nicknamed "Skin Flint." However, the fear of the fire and Mom's voice gave me the strength to do as she said.

It took just a half hour for that house to burn to the ground. The gathered crowd had carried multiple possessions out, but Donnie was the only thing that survived from the second floor. Mom soon came to get us from the yard corner, carrying a flannel table pad, which she tied on Donnie as a diaper. Some kind neighbor took us to the Vernon School to tell LaVon and Muriel what had happened. I remember that they were in tears as we rode home. I imagine Ellwood and Arleen had walked home since the rural school was close, and news had no doubt spread through the entire neighborhood. Beulah, Donnie and his father set up housekeeping in a small shed on that farm, while a neighbor offered our family a farm house which had not been lived in (expect for the multiple families of mice) for some time. Furniture appeared, but I don't remember who brought that, etc. People were very good to us, including our Grandpa Sandven who drove up one day with two big dolls dressed in a pink organdy dresses and bonnets, one each for Arleen and me since we had lost all of our toys in the fire.

EDUCATION 101

That fall, I started school, and walked daily to the neighborhood school with Ellwood and Arleen. I hated it! The school house was a small white frame building where children grades K-8 attended in the same room. The teacher was responsible for keeping the building warm in the winter, using a coal stove, keeping the building clean, pumping and bringing in a pail of well water every day, plus teaching the various levels of instruction. She also was responsible for arranging for and conducting at least one neighborhood program per year, etc. etc. etc. The teacher was strict, and since it was the time when kindergarten was just being introduced into the curriculum, I was given worksheet after worksheet to complete so as to finish the assigned work required for both kindergarten and first grade in the same year. The work was no problem, however, since my older sisters had often "played school" at home. But I had a new baby sister, and I suppose I had been knocked off that esteemed family status, which added to the frustration about school. Therefore, I often talked myself into "Not feeling good," so either Ellwood or Arleen would walk me home before the class time was up. After pulling that trick a couple of times, one day, Mom said to me, "O.K, You are sick! Sick people need to spend the day in bed so they can get better. I will bring you some soup at noon, but you will stay in bed all day today." I never begged to go home again unless I was really sick.

Our new baby, Patsy Lee, was chubby and cute. Ellwood promptly named her "Fat Boy." He also teased her that she really didn't belong to us since she had been the only one of Mom and Dad's seven children who had been born in a hospital, and he told her that he was sure they had mixed her up with another baby. That was pretty hard to believe as her baby picture was a "dead ringer" for Muriel's baby picture, and she, LaVon and I have been accused of being triplets in our advanced age.

We lived in the new house which the landlord built to replace the one that had been burned for less than two years, moving the next March to a farm closer to my first home. Somehow, Dad had secured a loan for 160 acres of good farm land which cost him $17,000. I was in second grade, so Arleen and I walked the two miles to our new school with the neighbor children who were close to our age. Of course, one of the parents might take us on days which were very cold, but most of the time, we walked. There was a rumor that a tramp had been seen in a small grove at the corner where we turned from the "Thor-Hardy" road onto the county road which led to our school. We never saw him, but we always quietly hurried past that section of our walk. Mom had told us stories of tramps coming to her house when she was growing up, asking for a meal. They were men who didn't have work for some reason or other, and were hungry and dirty, but not necessarily dangerous.

We had a good teacher in our new school, who accomplished the teaching/janitorial tasks efficiently for all the grades K-8. I had two boys in my class, Robert and Larry. Robert had been held back, and struggled with the work. Larry wasn't really sharp either, so it was easy to be the top of the class. I don't remember our teacher ever being outside with us at recess. That was her prep time, or time for her to feed the round heat stove with more wood in the winter. We wore layers in the winter, which I've resorted to again since moving to Minnesota. Our long underwear was under long brown stockings, since girls pretty much wore dresses all the time back then. When the weather started to get warmer in the spring, we unbuttoned the brown stockings from the garter belts, and rolled them down around our ankles. Muriel and LaVon became expert seamstresses and sewed most of our dresses. Patsy's and mine were often made over from one of the older girl's. We would beg to go with Dad when he shopped for chicken feed, because it came in flowered sacks, and we would choose ones with the design from which we wanted a dress to be made.

Our school yard had swings, a slide and a teeter totter. However, much of recess was spent making up our own games. We played the traditional "Ten Steps Around the House," "Red Light, Green Light," and "Pump Pump Pull Away." The school yard had many gopher holes, so someone invented the cruel game of "Drowning the Gophers." We would pump a pail of water, then, man the holes with baseball bats. One child would pour water down one of the holes, and when the gophers tried to escape, the "guard" at another hole would whomp him over the head. It almost makes me sick to think of that.

During class time, if we needed to use the bathroom, which was an outhouse behind the one room school house, we would raise one finger if we needed to pee, but if we needed a bowel movement, we raised two fingers, and would be excused to leave the room to take care of our needs. I never really understood the reason the teacher needed to know which bodily function we were to release, but now that I've had ample experience with children's tactics for getting out of class—

First school experience

Elain at 8 months (in rocking chair)

Grandpa Sandven's hogs

Pledging allegiance to flag at Lake #5 School

Elain holding baby sister, Patsy Lee

Baby Ronnie--the first grandchild in Mom's house

Sisters, Patsy and Elain in granite bath tub

Grandma Sandven and Aunt Emy

Proud Aunt Elain with Ronnie, Gary and Deanne--
Dad at left back by the house

Family Photo minus Ellwood who was in the army

Freshmen at Renwick Independent High School, Class of 1950

A Sunday afternoon at Grandma Sandvens

Part of Aunt Marie's family

Elain at age 5

Authenticated Record of Marriage

STATE OF IOWA,
Humboldt   County, } ss.

I, M.A. Wallukait , do hereby certify that I am the Clerk of the District Court in and for said County and State, and as such official I have the possession and control of official records of Marriages in and for said County and am charged with the duty of keeping said records; that in Book 8 of said marriage records, at Page 27 , is found and appears the following entry, to-wit:

FULL NAME OF GROOM Epharim C. Haaland *age 23*

Place of Residence Humboldt, Iowa Occupation Farmer

Age Next Birthday 24 Race or Color white

Place of Birth Humboldt County, Iowa

Father's Name Enoch Haaland

Mother's Maiden Name Enger Bigness

No. of Groom's Marriage 1st

Physician signing Groom's Certificate ------

Address -----

FULL NAME OF BRIDE Geneva Sandven *age 23*

Maiden Name if a Widow ------

Place of Residence Humboldt County, Iowa

Age Next Birthday 24 Race or Color white

Place of Birth Humboldt County, Iowa

Father's Full Name Magnus Sandven

Mother's Maiden Name Inger Olson

No. of Bride's Marriage 1st

Physician signing Bride's Certificate -------

Address -----

WHEN MARRIED March 10, 1921

Where Married Humboldt, Iowa

Witnesses Clarence Westre Bernice Michalson

By Whom Certified Rev. Thos B. Collins

Name and Office M.E. Pastor

Given under my hand and official seal on this 25th day of January , A. D., 19 57 .

[SEAL]

M.A. Wallukait
Clerk District Court.

By Ben Elliott
Deputy.

Form No. 753 FIDLAR & CHAMBERS CO., DAVENPORT, IOWA 59181

Mom and Dad's marriage certificate, duplicate copy

Humboldt Kosmos Print.

UNITED STATES OF AMERICA.

STATE OF IOWA, Humboldt County, ss.

BE IT REMEMBERED, That at a term of the *District* Court holden in and for said County, in the town of Dakota City therein, on the *11th* day of *September* in the year of our Lord one thousand eight hundred and ninety *five*, was present the Honorable *W B Quarton* sole presiding Judge of said Court, when the following among other proceedings were had, to-wit: *Magnus J Sandven*

a native of *Norway* and at present residing within said State, appeared in open Court, and makes application to be admitted to become a Citizen of the United States; and it appearing to the satisfaction of the Court, that he had declared on oath before *L R Baker Clerk District Court Humboldt County Iowa* a Court of Record, having common law jurisdiction, and using a seal, two years at least before his admission, that it was bona fide his intention to become a citizen of the United States, and to renounce forever all allegiance to any foreign Prince, Potentate, State or Sovereignty whatsoever, and particularly to *The King of Norway* of whom he was heretofore a subject; and said applicant having declared on oath, before this Court that he will support the Constitution of the United States, and that he doth absolutely and entirely renounce and abjure all allegiance and fidelity to every foreign Prince, Potentate, State or Sovereignty whatsoever, and particularly to *The King of Norway* of whom he was a subject.

The Court being satisfied that said applicant has resided within the United States for the term of five years next preceding his admission, without being at any time during the said five years out of the territory of the United States, and within this State one year at least; and it further appearing to the satisfaction of this Court that during this time he has behaved as a man of good moral character, attached to the principles of the Constitution of the United States and well disposed to the good order and happiness of the same. Thereupon the Court admitted the said applicant to become a citizen of the United States, and ordered all of the proceedings aforesaid to be entered of Record, which was accordingly done by the Judge of this Court.

IN TESTIMONY WHEREOF, I, *L R Baker* Clerk of the Court aforesaid, have hereto set my hand and affixed the Seal of the said Court, at my office in the town of Dakota City, in said County, this the *11th* day of *September* in the year of our Lord one thousand, eight hundred and ninety *five*

L R Baker .... Clerk.

Grandpa Sandven's naturalization certificate

Sandven family picture. Mom is on the far left

Farm on the Thor-Hardy Road where most of the stories took place

The Haaland children before Aunt Ida was born. Dad is on the far right

JOINING A LARGER SOCIETY

When technology became available in rural areas, our farm life became somewhat easier. It was a highlight in our life to get electricity and a telephone. I remember Mom's glee when we got our first refrigerator, eliminating countless trips to the cooling tank. We could then quit using kerosene and gas lamps, and eliminate the danger of tipping over a lamp and starting a fire.

Getting a telephone provided a lot of entertainment. Since we were on a "party line," we not only heard our special ring, but that of our neighbors as well. If we were bored and heard a neighbor's ring, we would listen in—making sure the others in our kitchen were being quiet so as to not be discovered "rubbering." If we needed to call out, we would ring a long single ring for the operator who would connect us to whom we wanted to call. It was not uncommon for the operator to visit a bit—ask about someone who was sick, or offer a bit of gossip. "Hacking" in its earliest form!

Our farming operation was forced into the "machine age" when Dad's horses and trusty team of mules broke down a fence and feasted on a rotting straw stack bottom. Even our pony, Dexter, was a victim of the tragedy. It was a sad day when the rendering truck drove into our yard and loaded the five bodies. Tears weren't usually a part of Mom's house, who coped with disappointment by telling us, "The Lord helps those who help themselves." But I don't remember her scolding any of us at that time, and a memory still sticks of seeing Ellwood watching out the window with tears streaming down his face. The horses were replaced with a steel wheeled Farmall tractor.

We still heated our house with a coal heating stove, however. It was a few years before we had a furnace or a gas stove. It was my job to gather cobs when I came home from school, so the coal fire could start easier. After the corn had dried sufficiently in the corn crib, and ear corn had been fed to the livestock, the cobs were rescued to be used to start a fire in the household stoves. Clean cobs were made if the corn had been put into a trough like device which was part of a small hand corn sheller. Dad or the hired man would turn a handle which powered the machine to shell the corn off the cobs. However, with the addition of tractor power, that process became modernized. When the corn had dried sufficiently in the corn crib, and/or the supply of shelled corn for the animals got low, Dad would alert the neighborhood man who owned the corn sheller to come to our farm. He would arrive with the large machine, and together the men would feed the ear corn into a large tray type opening. The tractor would power a large belt that ran from the tractor to the sheller, called a "power take off" and the ear corn would be gleaned off the cobs, which fell off to the side while the corn was powered up into a feed wagon. The huge pile of cobs would be shoveled into a farm wagon and unloaded into a small shed near our house called the cob house. I would get the "cob pail", go into the cob house, and fill it with cobs, then carry them into the house. Invariably, a mouse would jump out of the cob pile as I was filling the pail. I learned to make a loud noise by banging on the door to supposedly scare the mice into hiding. However, where were they to hide?? In the pile of cobs, of course!! One summer, Arleen and I made a makeshift playhouse between the cob house and the fence leading into the chicken yard. We made furniture from wooden crates that had carried staples home from the grocery store and spent many happy hours in that little space making and pretending to eat mud pies.

The upstairs in our house was heated by the heating stove which sat in a central place in our dining room. Small grates in the ceiling let the heat from that stove rise so the upstairs became quite comfortable.

It was relatively soon after the advent of our home's electricity that we also got water piped into the house. That meant water in the kitchen sink and an upstairs bathroom. Before that, we had used an outdoor toilet, or in the winter, we used a pot at night which had to be emptied daily. It sounds gross now, but we knew no difference as small children.

THE BIG GIRLS GROW UP

LaVon graduated high school at age sixteen. If there was a single enrollee in a certain class within the one room school, a student might be allowed to "skip a grade." LaVon had been a bright student, and it probably was thought to be efficient to move her into the next grade level work. Therefore, she attended a "teacher's training" program at the Iowa State Teacher's College at age seventeen. Even though Mom's own education had been limited, she wanted her children to be educated, and have a chance for a career. We were limited, however, to choices, because only the wealthy could afford to send their daughters to law or medical school, and that thinking was beyond our family's scope. Most girls became teachers, secretaries, nurses or farm wives. LaVon chose the latter, and married Leonard, the young neighbor who had helped us during the time of our fire. I came home from school one October day to find out that they had driven to Minnesota and been married that day. Mom and Dad had accompanied them since LaVon was not yet eighteen, and had to have her parent's signature. Patsy, at age three, had gone along since baby sitters weren't in our vocabulary at that time, and she was sporting a new ring!!! It seems she had made a scene when LaVon got a wedding ring, so Leonard had bought her one also. It must have been a cheapie, but I was jealous that she not only got to go to the wedding, but got a ring as well.

However, I liked Leonard, and he fit in as a second brother. He and LaVon had been married a bit over a year when they started having babies. I became an aunt to Ronnie at age ten. I assumed my role of babysitter with pride. One Sunday, we had arrived in church before LaVon and Leonard, and Ronnie spotted me sitting in the pew behind them as they became seated. He held out his baby arms and wouldn't rest until he was passed over the pew so I could hold him during the service.

Gary and Deanne were born in the following years, and since LaVon and Leonard farmed near Hardy as well, even though their farm was the opposite direction from the town, we saw them often. Babysitting those three beautiful kids was often my job. They also provided entertainment for our family. One summer day while their little family was shopping in Hardy, Mrs. McKim, an extremely large Hardy resident, had come walking down the street. Three year old Gary was standing in the back seat of their car near the open window. He started to sing in a very loud child's voice, "I don't want her, he can have her, she's too fat for me." I can still visualize Leonard throwing his head back and laughing when he told that story again and again.

I was a small, thin child. I was a finicky eater, and began to have constant leg aches. Mom decided I needed to have Doc Basinger look at me, and no doubt told him she thought I was anemic. I was. After that was determined, I was given some bad tasting liquid iron medicine. The first night that I was to take it right before meals, I was in the entry way near the sink. I couldn't swallow the bitter medicine, and promptly threw up! Most of the vomit went into Leonard's shoes which were standing near the sink. Sort of like his baptism into the family!

During that time, Muriel had also spent six weeks at Iowa State Teacher's College, in Cedar falls which is now UNI. That training had qualified her to teach. Her first job as teacher was in another nearby country school so she continued to live at home. Within her first year in that position, we had "the snow storm of a century." It began with a fury, and by the time Dad had picked up Arleen and I from our school, he realized he could not drive to get Muriel as well. So, he hitched our team of horses to the wagon, took some extra blankets with him, and rescued Muriel. Ellwood, who was a high school student in Vernon, spent the night sleeping on a mat on the gym floor, as the busses didn't dare attempt bringing the students home.

The car that I remember having for a very long time was a black Ford V8. We would all pile into it when we needed to go somewhere. Often, three people would need to sit in front, with an additional one on someone's lap if the whole family was in the car. We also had a Model B Ford which had been made into a pickup of sorts. Actually, the back seat had been removed and a wooden box was placed on the back chassis. Ellwood promptly named it the "chariot."

It was Dad's job to teach each of us to drive. When it was Arleen's turn, she, Patsy and I had gone to town with the family. Our farm yard was fenced to keep a few sheep that grazed on the weeds, etc. in tow. As we got to the gate, he got out, told Arleen to get into the driver's seat and drive through the gate. She over extended the wheel, and drove directly over the wire gate with Dad jumping out of the way. Patsy and I doubled over with laughter while Dad shouted, "I said, "drive THROUGH it not over it!"

We occasionally went on a shopping trip to Fort Dodge, and spent time at the Boston Store. No doubt, Mom had saved chicken money to buy us school shoes, etc. The Boston Store had an elevator, which really fascinated me. They also had a system where the clerk would place the money in a small brass receptacle, which would travel on a pulley type system to the main cashier, and if change was coming, it would be sent back to the clerk. Arleen had small feet, but they were wide. My feet were about as long as her's but they were very narrow, and I couldn't wear her hand me down shoes. Also, not all shoe companies made kids shoes in narrow widths, so my shoes could not be purchased from the Sears or Montgomery Ward catalogs, they had to be fitted in a shoe store, and were quite expensive. That caused a problem, since Mom's clothing budget was tight, and my shoes were often over that budgeted amount.

Ellwood didn't like to shop, and complained that Mom walked too fast while we walked through the streets, so one time, Mom bought him a pint of ice cream, which he ate while sitting in the car waiting for the female members of his family.

I had bought my first store bought dress with money I had earned from walking my neighbor's beans. That consisted of getting up early, having Dad sharpen the machete like corn knife, meeting two neighbor kids, and walking up and down the rows of the bean field. We cut out the cockleburs and the volunteer corn that appeared from last year's crop in that same field. I had done that at home as well, but loved working for the neighbor who paid us .90 per hour. Dad scolded me for accepting that much money, as he was sure the neighbor could not afford it. The shopping trip that allowed me to buy a red dress and pillbox hat to match was a highlight I remember well. I thought I was really dressed with class, but of course, I was not allowed to brag. No way would Mom want me to appear as a "poppa la hanna." That was her term for someone who pretended to be more than she felt he or she was in reality. When asked what it meant, she told us it was a Norwegian term for "paper rooster."

Another time, Patsy and I had seen some really cute skirts in a magazine or perhaps the Sears catalog. They were made from brown and white checked fabric trimmed in brown grosgrain ribbon. Oh, we thought, we'd really look good if we could have skirts like that. "Well," Mom said, "you girls know how to sew. If you catch a few of the hens that need to be culled because they are no longer laying, we will take them to town, sell them and you can buy the checked material and ribbon and make them." YUK!!!, I hated to go into the chicken house, and was sure I'd come out covered in mites, etc. etc. But at the same time, I really wanted a new skirt. So, I grabbed the chicken catcher and caught the hens. Mom often told the story that Elain thought that skirt was expensive because it was the hardest thing she had done to get something new. We wore those skirts even after laundering them faded the grosgrain ribbon onto the checks.

The only child that had a room of his own was Ellwood, so when he went to the army, it became Muriel's room, since she was a teacher, and the oldest. That's when Patsy and I started sharing a bed. It never donned on our mother to wake us in the morning gently, as I like yet today. She opened the stair door, and hollered, "GIRLS, IT'S TIME TO GET UP." She had made the rule that the last one to get up had to make the bed. Patsy would bound out of bed when I was still trying to open my eyes, go into the bathroom, sit down on the stool and sleep a few more minutes. By the time I would finally get up, make the bed, and go into the bathroom, she would still be there—sleeping. After several mornings, I complained to Mom about that rule not being fair since Patsy didn't really wake up—she just got up. Of course, The complaint did no good. Mom's response was, "Well, you can do that—just beat her at it tomorrow."

OUR PART IN THE WAR

Our country was at war in what is now called the "Great War." My family wasn't politically active, but they supported President Franklin D. Roosevelt as he led the country out of the great depression and through the great war. Every family was affected in some way. Ellwood anticipated joining the navy like many of his friends and his cousins, Russ and Donny Bygness. He went into a deep funk when he failed to pass the physical for admission into the navy. There was a spot discovered on his lungs, and it was assumed that at some time he had suffered from tuberculosis. I don't think that was ever confirmed in the years when a diagnosis was sometimes inaccurate. However, after a time, he was drafted into the army, and passed that physical. We proudly hung the blue star in our living room window, and felt like we were then doing our part.

Our trips to Kelling's grocery in Hardy took on a new perspective since we now had ration stamps for staples such as sugar and coffee. Gas was also rationed, which didn't particularly make a hardship on our family, since we seldom went very far in the car. But, with Ellwood in the army, stationed in Japan as an honor guard for General Douglas McArthur, we girls started doing tasks around the farm that had been his job. Mom did not drive a car, so when she and I took over the job of watering the pigs in a field down the road a ways, we would fill the tank that sat in the box of the chariot and I would drive down the road where Mom would get out to open the gate and we could get the job done. I was twelve, and it was pretty obvious that I was not old enough to drive on the road. After we had been doing that for several months, we noticed that the Highway Patrolman began making occasional trips down the Thor-Hardy road. We had heard that Larry Rasmussen, my classmate, had been picked up for driving without a license and Dad suspected that his father may have reported that I was also driving. So, it wasn't surprising that the patrol car came by just at pig watering time one afternoon. He stopped us, and before he could ask for the nonexistent license, Mom spoke up "It is my fault that Elain is driving on the road. We know it is not legal, but our son is in the army. I don't know how to drive, and since she and I have taken over this job to water our pigs it is necessary for her to drive." Did we get a ticket? I don't remember, but I will always remember Mom's confession and courage as she spoke.

Dad must have been pretty desperate for field help, because one day, he decided I should disc a field to get it ready to plant. I was proud that he had the confidence in me to drive the big tractor and do that, but I didn't know what to do when I came to a big pile of rocks in the middle of the field. Well, I thought, he would surely want the ground tilled right up to the rocks, so I slowed the throttle and drove over the rocks. Deep down in, I knew that was probably not the thing to do, but when I looked back at the disc, it didn't seem as if any of the blades were chipped. Maybe he won't ask about it, I thought! That didn't happen, and when he admitted he had forgotten to tell me about the rocks and asked what I did, he hit the roof when I told him I had gone over it. It was soon after that when a Hardy boy, LuVerne Claude, had finished his tour in the army and became employed as Dad's hired man.

When Ellwood returned from his time in the army, I was sixteen and pretty well grown up. I had been a kid when he left, so when he returned, we had more in common. He would often take me to the movies if he couldn't find a friend to share that activity. One time, when I was a junior in high school, he transported me to a ball game at my school. Sammy Green, my high school boyfriend, had just gotten his driver's license and was permitted to drive his Dad's 1939 Chevy. He asked to take me home, and of course, I said yes. I could tell Ellwood was disgusted when I went to tell him my plans. He hit the roof when I came home, and I knew if he took me to some event—maybe at Mom and Dad's suggestion, it was NOT permissible for me to take another ride back home.

EDUCATION 102

When the teacher left Lake #5, our school, there was an opening for a new teacher. Dad had been elected "director" of that township. It still seems a bit odd to me that Muriel was thought to be the right teacher for our school. I was then in the fifth grade, and if I have one remaining grudge against my parent's action, it was that they thought it was OK for Muriel to be my teacher as well as the dominate big sister at home. I was expected to be the "model student," and I was—knowing that if I was not, I would suffer both at home as well as at school. Patsy started school during Muriel's three years in that school, and tells a story of wetting her pants because Muriel had "tattled" to Mom that she was interrupting too much. After a severe scolding from Mom, she knew she couldn't ask to go to the outdoor privy during class time. Another time, my classmate, Larry, had played a trick on her, and she was frustrated because she didn't know who had done it. That night, she complained to Mom that I knew and wouldn't tell her. Mom finally gave in, and said I had to tell her who had done the deed. I didn't learn to appreciate Muriel until we were both adults and I recognized her many talents and felt that she was proud of me.

Muriel's reign as our teacher ended when she applied and got a job teaching first and second grade at Vernon Consolidated. I had finished seventh grade, and was looking forward to a new teacher. Teachers were very scarce because the Great War had taken most of the qualified women to work in factories, etc. The government approved a "teacher training" program which allowed young women to attend a "normal training" two year program during their last two years of high school. Since it wasn't implemented as part of the Vernon school, Arleen spent two years living in a rented room in Eagle Grove so she could participate in that program. While there, she became good friends with Mavis Ellertson, who became my teacher at her ripe age of seventeen. Arleen got a job in a school a few miles away, and we often heard stories of the escapades of the "big boys" who were her pupils, and were much taller than her. One of them was only a year or so younger than her as well. Arleen taught only that one year, but Mavis made teaching her career for several years.

I overheard Muriel telling Mavis that I was a good student, even though she had NEVER given me an indication that she believed that. Of course, she too, had been cautioned about being a papa la hanna, and I'm sure that included not contributing to my becoming one. Mavis had never attended a rural school, and even though she was trained??, she was pretty lost when it came to handling a schedule that included teaching several grades at the same time. Since Robert had moved, and Larry had dropped out of school, I was the lone eighth grader, and the other children were at least four years younger than me. I swear that was the year I decided to become a teacher, since in reality, I had taught the younger children in several ways. However, Mavis was determined that I would be amply prepared for the eighth grade exams, which were held in the court house in Dakota City in Humboldt County. She drilled me with the exam preparation booklets, and on the day or the exams, I felt I had done well. We were to find out the results in three weeks. On the Saturday before the results were to be made known, Muriel called Miss Messer to see how I had done. (Frances Messer was the county superintendent of rural schools. Muriel had become acquainted with her as a result of her teaching experience.) She appeared shocked when she was told that I had an overall score of

93% which was the highest in the county. I, too, was in disbelief, and was not shocked when Muriel told Mom, in my presence, that it was a pretty dumb class overall. Being at the top of the class required me to give a speech at the 8th grade graduation ceremony. It was scheduled to immediately follow the part of the program where several of us had performed the "Virginia Reel" on stage. I was very short of breath, and panted between the words of my speech. I was embarrassed by that, but found comfort in that I thought I looked good, since I had worn one of my very first store bought dresses. It was a pink linen flared skirt with a pink printed silky top with large shoulder pads.

After that eighth grade graduation, I was ready for "high school." It was a bit scary to board the school bus. By this time, there had been some redistricting, and we no longer were in the Vernon Consolidated School District. I was the first Haaland child to attend Renwick Independent High School. I had been in 4H with Phyllis, one of my classmates who welcomed me in the new experience. Mardelle Larson had only been with that class for one year, so she and I became the "new girls." Neither of us was athletically inclined, and we were elected as cheer leaders. We became fast friends, and since our "one car family" could have limited my after school activities, I often spent overnights at her home. She was an only child, and her parents were more than good to me. Her father was the depot agent, which meant his family lived upstairs in the railroad depot. A train went through in the middle of every night. I suppose it woke me the first night, but I quickly learned to ignore it, and it never bothered my sleep.

We gathered every morning in the assembly hall, which served as the "home room" for the entire high school student body. Remember, there were only seventeen students in my class, and that was a typical class size. The principal would address us each day before leaving for the first period class. While in class we sat in alphabetical order. Since I was the only person whose last name began with H, I was seated next to Howard Gillespie, who was the principal's son. He had done chores before coming to school each day, and those chores included milking their family's cow, so he smelled a bit like the cow barn. However, "Gus" and I became best friends. We confided in each other about most everything, especially if one of us had boy/girlfriend troubles. Gus was not an athlete, and the after school practices would have conflicted with his farm activities, so he became a cheer leader along with another boy, Mardelle and me. One Sunday afternoon, he and Sammy, my boyfriend, drove out to our farm in Gus' pickup, and I went for a ride with them. No hanky panky, just a leisurely fun ride, but Mom let me know in no uncertain terms that I was NOT to ever to go with TWO boys again. She did not understand that Gus was never that kind of a boyfriend.

Our superintendent was also our math teacher. I believe he was one of the best. I loved his algebra class, because he explained it to give it meaning to our lives. I also loved the Home Ec class and Mrs. Rossman, who was a young teacher at that time. I already knew how to sew, so when we had the semester of sewing, it was easy to be the head of the class. I had taught everyone in the class how to make hand sewn buttonholes, and when it came time to draw for the practical part of the final exam, I drew the slip that said, "Make a handmade buttonhole." Rita Mae Rossman thought it was hilarious! I did not like the typing class or the economics class, which are probably the two that I use the most today, but at the time, I didn't think I'd use either in my adult life.

I always liked to sing, and since my parents could not afford a musical instrument, I didn't have a chance to be in the band—only Patsy got that privilege as they were a bit more financially secure by the time she reached the age of making that choice. Anyway, I was in Glee Club, Mixed chorus, Girl's Sextet and sang solos in the music contest in the spring. One day in Glee Club, as our teacher was having us warm up by vocalizing "ooo" up and down the scale, Phyllis and I, seated together, started singing poo and got the giggles. We laughed and laughed and were finally sent back to the assembly. Being sent out of class was the ultimate in punishments, but we thought it was funny, and had to stand in the hall to compose ourselves before we could enter the room. Four of us formed a mixed quartet as well, and even sang at high school commencement when we were juniors in high school. Those events plus having to attend the athletic events to lead the cheering, filled up my social calendar pretty well, and I loved it. Being thought of as the Larson's second daughter allowed me to do those things. I regret that I don't think I ever properly thanked Mardelle's parents for their kindness.

Once a month, we had a school dance. Mr. Gillespie loved to dance, and since his wife had died, he attended the dances along with Gus. No doubt, his role there was to be a chaperone, but I always suspected that he came because he loved to dance. I made my own prom dresses, and wore them with pride. We did not have to have dates to attend the prom. I remember one that Phyllis and I attended together and had a wonderful time.

We got a new superintendent when I was a senior in high school. Cultural mores were changing, and he decided that the girls in his school should wear skirts. I was the first girl who challenged that new yet unannounced rule, although there were rumors floating around that we would soon be told. I arrived in school wearing blue jeans, and was called into his "esteemed office" to listen to his rationale that girls should wear skirts to school. He did declare Fridays as "girls wearing jeans day." I never liked that man, and missed the former superintendent who had been my favorite math teacher.

MOVING ON

When Larry Lerdal returned home from serving in the army, he and Muriel were married. They were also farmers and lived in the area of Goldfield, which wasn't far from us. By that time, Patsy was old enough to help, so she and I shared baby sitting with Carol, when she was born to them. Their second baby, Scott, was born when Carol was about two or three years old, and she stayed at our house while Muriel was in the hospital. It had been decided that Carol should go with her father when he picked up her Mom and new baby brother. Patsy and I were to go along and watch Carol while Larry went into the hospital to retrieve the new mom and son. Patsy and I bickered a lot, and weren't always kind to one another. While driving home, after we had oohed and awed over Scott, Carol was standing between Patsy and me in the back seat. One of us said something she didn't like, and she said in a loud voice, "TUT UP." Patsy and I thought it was hilarious, and burst into giggles. That was Carol's clue that she had found a way to entertain her aunts, so she kept chanting, "TUT UP, "TUT UP." The more she said it, the more we laughed. Muriel's backward glances toward us were those of pure disgust.

Joining 4H was another welcome event. My 4H leader was a skilled homemaker, and since we had such limited transportation, I was occasionally welcomed to her home, as her daughter Phyllis was my age. If we were to participate in some event that required early morning arrival, I would spend the night at Mrs. Lane's home. She also expected her children to help with chores, and used a term that I sometimes used later with my own children. We were instructed to use "Going Away Speed."

Mom was proud of what I learned in 4H, and I remember her telling someone that her girls had not only learned to be better seamstresses and used better cooking skills; they had learned to speak in front of groups, a skill she wished she had possessed.

Marilyn Gangstead and I became a team for 4H demonstration purposes. We learned how to iron men's shirts with a lot of skill, and after presenting it at the county fair, and winning a blue ribbon, we were asked to present it as programs for service clubs in the community. It was at such an event that Norman first learned who I was, as he was being honored for some 4H achievement at the same meeting where Marilyn and I taught those men how to iron their own shirts. We won the top award at the county fair, but we weren't old enough to participate in state fair competition. The following year, Mrs. Lane suggested we do a similar ironing presentation only adjusting it so that it would educate home seamstresses the skill of pressing seams as the garment would be in construction. We introduced different kinds of pressing cloths, pressing hams, etc. Now, we were old enough, and our prize was a trip to the state fair. We would stay in the makeshift dormitory for a full week. We were chaperoned, of course, by one of Arleen's friends, Jeanette Korslund. She appeared quite nervous about the task. We were both shy farm girls who were very cautious, and sneaking out at night with strange boys was the farthest thing from our minds. I don't remember what placing we got with our demonstration on the state level, so I don't think it was the top, but we had a good time, and it did a lot to cement our friendship. There was a talent show, with the contestants being 4H members, and Marilyn accompanied me as I sang, "Hi, Ho, Come to the Fair," from the then current movie "State Fair."

Arleen was accepted into nurses training at Fairview Hospital in Minneapolis when she turned eighteen. Her move to the city gave a new perspective to my life. Since I was having a blast in my new experience of high school with my friends, I did not visit often. However, when she met Ralph Enzmann and became engaged to him, I was thrilled to become their maid of honor. I was excited when they invited me to visit them before they moved to take their first jobs in International Falls. I had called the Fort Dodge airport to find out when the plane would leave, and assumed that is all that I had to do. Well, when Dad drove me to the airport on the specified morning, we were told that the plane was full, and no one could just show up, there had to have been reservations. Therefore, we had to find a pay phone, call Arleen and Ralph and explain that I would not be coming into the MSP airport, but they should rather meet me at the bus station. They were invited to a wedding that would occur during my visit, so I should bring appropriate clothing. I had made a new dress. Pink organdy!! I can see it yet—not because it looked good, but because it embarrasses me to remember how I must have looked. No doubt organdy had been chosen because it was affordable. It also was "see through" and it wrinkled badly. I had bought a pink slip with lots of tan lace, which made the dress somewhat opaque!!! There were tucks in the bodice, thank goodness, and a full, much wrinkled skirt that was cinched with a self-fabric belt held together by pinning on a small spray of pink fabric roses. I didn't know Ralph well, since our trips to Minneapolis had been few and far between, but I certainly gained a great respect for him at that event. Arleen was a friend of the bride, and had the honorable task of serving the coffee at the reception. Ralph escorted me like he was proud to introduce his new sister in law to his friends, even though I know now that I looked like a mess.

EDUCATION 201

My high school graduation was bitter sweet. The seventeen classmates had been my "launching pad" to friendships outside of my family, and I loved them dearly. We vowed that we would meet every five years, and amazingly most of us continue to do that to this day.

I was anxious for the next chapter of my life to begin. Marilyn and I both decided to go to Waldorf College in Forest City, Iowa. We had decided not to room together, but we knew we would be friends there as well as at home, and we were. Mom and Dad had scheduled a rare outing for the weekend when I was supposed to leave for school, leaving Ellwood at home to transport me and my stuff. Well, Ellwood thought girls going to college was a waste of money, and that I would just go there to find a husband, get married, and not use my education.

To vent his frustration, I believe, more than needing the help, I had to help him sort hogs on Saturday before leaving on Sunday. It was my job to hold a large, heavy wooden gate to prevent the herded hogs from going back into the pasture. That was fine until ten or more two hundred pound animals came roaring at the gate. I dropped it and darted to safety. Many of you who read this will remember your Uncle Ellwood's demeanor when he was mad. It was not a pleasant drive to Forest City the next day.

To my surprise, I was terribly homesick those first weeks at Waldorf. I was assigned a roommate who was a year ahead of me, and liked to sleep. I wanted to be out and about, and from early on, I knew she and I would not become friends. Marilyn and I both tried out for the big choir and neither of us made it until later in the year. I had been a top student in all my years of education, and it was pretty clear that I had stiff competition. So, at the end of two weeks, when I went home for the weekend, I told Mom I wasn't sure I wanted to go back. I don't remember the exact words, but the tone was, "You were anxious to go-we are sacrificing to let you go, you will go and stay there." I knew that it was time for me to vacate Mom's house. By Christmas, I couldn't have been paid to quit school and I knew Mom had been right! Again!